YOUR KNOWLEDGE HAS VALUE

Bibliographic information published by the German National Library:

The German National Library lists this publication in the National Bibliography; detailed bibliographic data are available on the Internet at http://dnb.dnb.de .

Imprint:

Copyright © 2012 GRIN Verlag, Open Publishing GmbH
Print and binding: Books on Demand GmbH, Norderstedt Germany
ISBN: 9783656413486

This book at GRIN:

http://www.grin.com/en/e-book/213057/interpretation-and-intertextuality-of-the-film-the-matrix

Marius Gerschau

Interpretation and Intertextuality of the film "The Matrix"

GRIN Publishing

GRIN - Your knowledge has value

Since its foundation in 1998, GRIN has specialized in publishing academic texts by students, college teachers and other academics as e-book and printed book. The website www.grin.com is an ideal platform for presenting term papers, final papers, scientific essays, dissertations and specialist books.

Visit us on the internet:

http://www.grin.com/

http://www.facebook.com/grincom

http://www.twitter.com/grin_com

Marius Gerschau, Q12   05.11.2012

HCA-Gymnasium Sulzbach-Rosenberg

W-Seminar "Film Analysis"

Interpretation and Intertextuality of the film
"The Matrix"

Table of Contents

1. Introduction

Take a trip down memory lane and find yourself in the year 1999. This year marked the birth of a film that would eventually become one of the most praised science fiction films of all time. Not only being received positively by critics and having a worldwide gross profit of over 463 million dollars with a budget of 63 million dollars, *The Matrix* by the Wachowski Brothers quickly gained a cult following for it's highly professional fighting scenes, revolutionary special effects and steampunk atmosphere. It spawned two even more successful and anticipated sequels four years later, three video games, comic books and an anime spin-off. But what really made *The Matrix* a mentionable film was not it's focus on action scenes, but it's complex storyline and a wide range of possible Interpretation and Intertextuality. This seminar paper will give you a glimpse of how far those two points can reach. It will summarize the plot of *The Matrix* first, then it will interpret the points in the movie, that seem unclear and confusing to the viewer and last but not least explain the most notable references and the Intertextuality to works, that inspired the movie. It will, however, only treat the first and original movie *The Matrix* and not it's sequels *Matrix Reloaded* and *Matrix Revolutions* and other media from the franchise.

2. The Plot

The Matrix revolves around Thomas Anderson in the year 1999, who lives a double life as an employee for a software company at daytime, as well as a criminal hacker under the pseudonym "Neo" at nighttime to earn money. He doesn't seem to go out and enjoy himself very much and when not at work, he desperately searches for the meaning of the so called "Matrix" and a man who could lead him to its answers called Morpheus. One night, after he fell asleep on his computer, sentences about the Matrix and an instruction saying "Follow the white rabbit."(min 7) appear on his computer screen and seem to be able to predict certain events, just like someone knocking at his door. After opening the door for a customer of his hacked data business, he is told by the buyer to go out with him and his friends for the sake of Neo's health. At first slightly excited about this idea, he recognizes a tattoo of a white rabbit on the shoulder of one of the customers friends and decides to "follow the white rabbit"(min 7) and go with them.

After going to a club with this crew he meets a woman called Trinity, who is, just like Neo, an infamous hacker on the Internet and seems to know a lot about Neo. She tells him that he is in danger and that she went through the same questioning about the

Matrix and Morpheus once in order to find the answers. The next morning, at his work cubicle, he receives a package containing a cellphone, which immediately rings. The caller is Morpheus, through whom he discovers, that he is prosecuted by three agent looking men in this very moment. Morpheus tries to guide Neo through the cubicles to help him escape but he still gets captured by the agents, who arrest him.

In an interrogation room, they reveal, that they know about his second life and the crimes he committed. They offer to delete his crime file, if Neo tells them about Morpheus, who is considered the most dangerous man alive by the agents. Neo refuses to cooperate by flipping them off and demanding a phone call. He then strangely loses control over his mouth, which seems to disappear. After that, the agents implant a strange device into his belly button, which causes Neo to wake up in his room, holding the events for a dream. He then gets called by Morpheus again, who tells him once again, that he is in high danger and the first time, that he is supposed to be "the One" and that Morpheus has been looking for him his entire life. He also tells him a meeting point under a bridge.

Upon arriving, Neo gets picked up by Trinity and several unknown people, who all seem to be affiliated with Morpheus. They point a gun at him in their car and tell him to take his shirt off in order to remove the bug the agents have planted in him with a strange device. Neo struggles, whether he should trust them and considers getting out of the car, but Trinity appeals to Neo's curiosity about the Matrix. He stays in the car and Trinity removes the bug. He meets Morpheus at his home then. After talking about various issues like Fate, Slavery and "the Truth", which doesn't seem to have much context at all, he tells Neo, that the Matrix is basically everywhere, but you can't be told what it is, you have to witness it to understand it.

He offers Neo one of two pills: A blue pill, which will make Neo accept his fate and never understand what the Matrix is and a red one, which will show Neo what it is, but he couldn't go back then. He chooses and swallows the red one and is told to follow Morpheus into the next room, where some kind of laboratory with Morpheus' crew is. Neo is told to sit down and recognizes a mirror, which is broken but seems to fix itself after a while on its own. After touching the mirror, Neo's world begins to fade and he seems to start hallucinating, while Morpheus asks him, whether he ever had a dream that was so real, that he couldn't figure what was real and what was not (min 30).

With this last words, Neo wakes up in a strange kind of booth filled with liquid, with a lot of wires attached to various plugs on his body being completely naked and having no hair at all. He gets rid of the wires and realizes, that there are millions of those kind of booths around him. He then gets sucked out of his booth and lands in a sea, where a big crane rescues him. After his arrival he meets Morpheus and his crew again, is introduced by Morpheus by the words "Welcome to the real world"(min 33) and blacks out.

After regaining consciousness he notices, that the crew started to do various operations to his body, to strengthen his muscles. After asking Morpheus, why his eyes hurt so much, he is told, that he never used them before. After his physical abilities are fully recovered, he is told by Morpheus, that the actual year is rather 2199 than 1999 and that they are currently on Morpheus futuristic hovercraft ship, the Nebuchadnezzar. He reintroduces his crew to Neo, which consists of Trinity, several other members he saw before and a few new ones.

To finally explain to him what the Matrix is, Neo is sit down in a dentist like stool where he gets jacked to a machine into a plug in the back of his head. Immediately after that he finds himself in a completely empty room with Morpheus, who tells him, that they are currently in a computer program. Neo's clothing and hair is different than before and he lacks his plugs and he struggles over the question whether some of the newly spawned furniture is real or not, which is not. Morpheus tells Neo that the world that he knew as the world in 1999 is only a computer simulation called the Matrix and the real world is a dark post-apocalyptic desert full of ruins somewhere around the end of the 22nd century.

Early in the 21st century, mankind was able to create Artificial Intelligence, which resulted in the creation of a race of machines. Soon a war between humans and machines began and the human race obscured the sky to defeat the machines, who relied on solar power at that point. To survive, the machines started to use humans as their energy source and used them as a form of battery, where also Neo was seen after awaking from the Matrix previously. They began cultivating humans in large fields and invented the Matrix to make them believe, that they were living a normal live while they were used as batteries. Neo refuses to believe all of this and wakes up on the stool back in the Nebuchadnezzar, where he panics and pukes before blacking out once again.

Being fully aware of his situation, Neo is told by Morpheus of a man who was born inside the Matrix, "who had the ability to change whatever he wanted, [...] it was he, who freed the first of us, who taught us the truth. [...] After he died, the Oracle prophesied his return and that his coming would hail the destruction of the Matrix, end the war (and) bring freedom to our people..."(min 43). He tells Neo that he and others searched their entire lives for his reincarnation within the Matrix and that he freed Neo from it, because he thinks that he is "the One".

After this he is introduced to the Nebuchadnezzar's operator Tank, who was born in Zion, the last city in the real world inhabited by humans, who are not part of the slavery of the machines and offer resistance. He learns several combat techniques like Ju Jitsu, Tae Kwon Do or Kung Fu, merely by Tank loading programs into his brain. Neo and Morpheus test his new abilities in a virtual sparring program, where Neo is told, that he can bend certain rules within this virtual world and in the Matrix. To further this point, Neo tries the "jump program" where he should manage to jump between two skyscrapers, like Morpheus is already able to do. He fails, falls on the concrete and wakes up from the program, realizing that he is bleeding from his mouth a little bit. He is told that although nothing within programs is actually real, injuries and death would also have damaging or lethal consequences in the real world for "the body can't live without the mind."(min 53)

The next lesson he learns with the aid of another training program is that there are sentient programs within the Matrix called the Agents. They are highly dangerous, indestructible, have superhuman speed and strength and the ability to spawn everywhere, also in humans who have not been freed from the Matrix's system. They serve as the machines way to eliminate troublemakers like Morpheus and other rebels. To destroy the Matrix, those Agents have to be defeated first, which is not possible by anyone, except Neo when he will realize his powers.

Meanwhile in the real world the Nebuchadnezzar has to deal with a bunch of hostile machines, which task is to find and destroy rebellious groups. The crew manages to get rid of them, without using their EMP-weapon, which kills any electric activity within a certain radius, but also the Nebuchadnezzar's.

Neo then meets the Crew's member Cypher, who regrets the decision of taking the red pill and getting unplugged from the Matrix and is skeptical of Neo being "the One". Furthermore he made a deal with one of the Agents within the Matrix to forget the whole truth about it and being able to live a normal life in the Matrix again. In compensation therefor, he has to hand over Morpheus to the Agents, which would mean the end of Zion, because he knows the access codes for it's mainframe.

While the rest of the crew is unaware of that deal, they all prepare to go into the Matrix, to show Neo to the Oracle, so she can decide, whether he is "the One" or not.

The Oracle once told Morpheus that he would find "the One", that's why he is rather optimistic, but after actually talking to her, Neo is convinced that he is not. The Oracle also says, that Morpheus believes in Neo so much, that he would sacrifice himself for his sake one day.

After his audience, the whole crew prepares to exit the Matrix once again, which happens through a fixed telephone, but Neo witnesses a Deja-Vu, which happens when the Matrix is changed and a squad of police forces followed by some Agents begin to storm the building they are in. During the escape from that building through the walls, Morpheus gets beat up and captured by an Agent in order to rescue Neo. The crew then tries to exit the Matrix, but Cypher, who managed to exit first, kills Tank and his brother Dozer in the real world with a plasma rifle. He argues with Trinity over the Matrix and that he feels like a slave in the real world, and begins to unplug and consequently kill every crew member except Neo and Trinity. Just as he tries to do the same thing with Neo, he gets shot and killed by Tank who survived the incident. He releases both back into the real World.

Meanwhile in the Matrix, the Agents, leaded by an Agent called Smith, try to get Zion's access codes by breaking into Morpheus mind. Being aware, that this would be fatal for the whole resistance, Tank decides to pull his plug and kill Morpheus, but Neo, who knew that this situation would happen for his sake, decides to go into the Matrix and rescue Morpheus, who is on top of a military secured skyscraper guarded by three Agents.

With a lot of guns, Neo and Trinity begin to storm and shoot through the whole building. On top of the skyscraper, they encounter an Agent and for the first time, Neo is able to move with superhuman speed and dodge the Agents bullets. They manage to shoot him and rescue Morpheus with a helicopter and a minigun, with Neo once again showing his advanced powers. After having Morpheus fully secured, they order Tank to locate an exit, but while Morpheus and Trinity are able to exit the Matrix, an Agent destroys the phone providing it. After a fight with Agent Smith, Neo manages to escape and searches for a new exit guided by Tank in a flat, with the Agents following him.

Meanwhile in the real world, the Nebuchadnezzar is once again attacked by machines, which means that the EMP would be useless, as it would mean Neo's death while he is still in the Matrix. On his escape from the Agents, Neo gets shot multiple times by Agent Smith causing his death. In the real world, where the attack of the machines becomes critical, Trinity tells Neo's body that he has to be "the One", for the

Oracle told her that she would fall in love with "the One". With this confession, Neo resurrects and is able to stop the Agents bullets and to kill Agent Smith. Just as the machines almost arrive the crew, Neo manages to exit the Matrix and the crew fires the EMP to immobilize the machines.

The film ends with Neo declaring war to the machines through a telephone booth, before flying into the sky, demonstrating that he is "the One".

3. Explanation

Although the scenario of our world merely being a dream world and the real world being a post apocalyptic wasteland is explained rather well in *The Matrix*, there are some questions about the film that remain blurry to nonsensical. The film may show a scenario that is a little bit far-fetched and cliche, but everything could happen in our world as well with the premise of an existing Artificial Intelligence, but there are some points that don't fit into the rather logical setting. For example, who is the Oracle and what role does she play? How is Neo able to do things others couldn't, just because he's "the One"? And who is "the One" at all and what's so special about him, to break all the rules he wants? This chapter will take a deeper look into the setting of *The Matrix* to understand the most crucial elements in the film and take a look at how deep the "rabbit hole"(min 28) really goes.

3.1. Extended Definition of the Matrix

To fully understand how certain processes, like Neo and the rest of the rebels bending the rules of the Matrix, work, you have to understand the Matrix itself first. You have to understand how humans are connected to the Matrix and how them interacting with it works. You may think after watching the movie, that there are two worlds within the franchise. This is true, but not entirely.

First of all, you have to stop looking at the Matrix as a physical world. It is nothing but a virtual world and doesn't exist per se, that means it could be duplicated and changed whenever the machines do so. This rule is not transferable to the real world. This is why you can't say that there are two worlds, but you can say there is one world and a virtual one. One that exists and one that doesn't.

So how do humans interact within the Matrix? Is the Matrix one big space and every human controls a "virtual I" through he sees the Matrix? It is comparable with an multiplayer computer game, which the Matrix basically is (although a rather advanced one). In order to play, you need to install the game on your computer first, the virtual worlds are rendered and exist on every computer simultaneously and the multiplayer servers only recognize the players actions and redirect them to other ones, they do not build a general world where every player can access. This is also how the Matrix works. Every human has his own copy of the Matrix on his brain, there is no general Matrix anywhere(comp. Lawrence 8).

This is a crucial realization, because this shows, that everything that happens in the Matrix just happens in someone's brain, just like a dream. Injuries and the death in the real world as a result of injuries and death in the Matrix are explained that the brain, or to be precise the subconscious of an individual is not able to distinguish this highly realistic illusion from reality ("Your mind makes it real" min 53). In a conclusion you could say, that everything that happens within in someone's Matrix, happens only in someone's thoughts, that is why it is not real at all.

3.2 Bending the Matrix

Knowing this, you can also explain, how exactly Neo, Morpheus and the others bend the rules of the Matrix. Like in a lucid dream, once you realize that you are asleep, or in the Matrix, that you are not witnessing reality, you are able to do whatever you want, like going through walls or flying. But why are Morpheus, Trinity and the others not able to do whatever they want and can only bend a few rules? The key to this question is, that although they know, that they are in a virtual world, their brains can't fully accept this, they are still doubting subconsciously (comp Lawrence 15). A lucid dream is rather easy to distinguish from reality, that's why the state of being aware that you are not witnessing reality is achieved rather easily. But the Matrix is such a realistic illusion, that the brain has problems to accept the fact that nothing is real. This is why Neo is able to bend every rule he wants. He and his subconscious have fully understood the unreal nature of the Matrix at the end of the film, while the others have not (comp Lawrence 15).

3.3. The Oracle

Now let's take a look at the Oracle. Throughout the whole film *The Matrix* it is never defined clearly who the Oracle is at all. Although she is depicted omniscient and able to predict the future for the viewer, everything she says is rather cryptic and blurry. Neo leaves the Oracle with knowing that he is not "the One" and that either he or Morpheus would die, because of Morpheus' faith towards Neo. But if you follow the film, you can see clearly that none of those predictions becomes true. So what's the point of the

Oracle, when none of what she said makes sense to the viewer? Is she a regular human still jacked to the Matrix who likes to talk a lot or is she a omniscient program?

It is more likely that she is none of these both, she is too old to be a regular human, because she existed since the beginning of the resistance and the existence of a program, hostile towards the machines in a world that was entirely created by the machines is also rather unlikely. The scene with the Oracle begins with Neo entering her flat and he sees, that he is not the only potential "One" (min 71 ff.). There are several children, who are waiting for their audiences and Neo begins talking to a boy, who is able to bend spoons only by looking at them. He tells Neo, that he has to realize the truth, that there is no spoon, and that not the non-existing spoon bends but only Neo himself bends the image of this non-existing spoon, for everything that happens in the Matrix only happens in his mind.

This little scene suggests who the Oracle really is, she is only a projection of Neo's and all the others, who were with the Oracle, fears and subconscious feelings. This is how Neo unknowingly bends the appearance of the Matrix the first time, he projects those feelings onto a person he can talk with. This explains why the Oracle does nothing but telling Neo what he already knows, or fears. That means when she tells Neo "that's why she (Trinity) likes you"(min 70), he only realizes his feelings towards her and the statement "Sorry kid. You got the gift, but it looks like you're waiting for something."(min 72) only reflects his doubts he still has of being "the One", she never actually tells him, that he is not "the One". Morpheus believes a 100 percent that he would find "the One" someday, that's why the Oracle, his subconscious, told him, that he would find him for sure ("That I would find the One" min 67). The Oracle, like the rest of the Matrix, doesn't really exist, but that is not really important for the rest of the plot, as she has a guiding function for almost everybody in the film.

3.4. Neo as "the One"

So far almost every crucial point has been explained, even how Neo's special powers work. But there is still one point, that does not fit into this setting: the existence of "the One", a human with superhuman powers, that he has from birth, who would be able to end the war between humans and machines once and for all on his own. This seems way more than cliche to fit into the rather authentic setting, because it would suggest, that there would be a supernatural component in the movie, which is considered Science Fiction, not Fantasy. So you have to ask yourself, whether Neo actually is "the One" at the end of *The Matrix* and if such an entity really exists.

What differs "the One" from a "mere" human are the powers that he possesses and those powers come with fully understanding that the Matrix is not real at all, as described in Chapter 3.2. But why did just Neo reach this insight of all people, was he really born to be "the One" ? To reach the state of being aware, that you don't live reality within the Matrix, you have not only to convince yourself, but also your subconscious of this fact (see Chapter 3.2). Throughout the whole film, there are hints, that being "the One" has actually to do something with believing in yourself and not a birth given gift. "I'ma let you know a little secret: being "the One" is just like being in love, no one can tell you you're in love you just know it, through and through, balls to bones."(min 71) and "You remember, you don't believe in any of this fate crap, you're in control of your own."(min 74) are two statements by the Oracle, that suggest exactly, that being "the One" has nothing to do with fate, it comes from believing in yourself and believing that you can bend the Matrix, but that also suggests, that the existence of a supernatural being like "the One" is not real and that theoretically everyone could reach the state of "the One".

But why did only Neo, what's so special about him? Neo has something that others have not: that a lot of people, like Morpheus, Trinity, Tank and the rest of the crew, minus Cypher, believe in him being "the One" and consequently boosting his self-confidence. This self-confidence affects his subconscious in a way, that it can accept "the Truth" of the Matrix much easier, because this is triggered by merely believing and self-confidence helps you in believing in yourself. But that is not everything. The key of Neo being "the One", is his resurrection at the end of the film. After Neo died in the Matrix, but still being alive in the real world, he still witnesses Trinity's words and kiss and he fully understands that although he thinks he dies, that he is actually absolutely alive (comp Lawrence 15).

This is the crucial point, where he is different than the others: He had to witness death within the Matrix first to fully see, that nothing is real within the Matrix (comp Lawrence 16). If he can die within the Matrix and resurrect afterwards and so create a paradox, he can also dodge bullets paradoxically or fly through the air. In a conclusion you could say, that almost everything in *The Matrix* can be explained with one simple word: "believe" or to cite the Oracle "Know Thyself"(min 70).

4. Intertextuality

Now that *The Matrix* has been interpreted, let's take an even deeper look at the film. While Chapter 3 explains the movie within it's setting, this chapter will take it outside and have a look at some religious and philosophical symbols and other myths and works that inspired and are suggested throughout the movie.

4.1. Biblical Approaches

A lot of similarities and references between the new testament and the film are found throughout the movie. First of all, Neo's path through the film is very similar to the path of Jesus Christ. Neo serves as the messiah, who frees the whole humanity. He has superhuman powers, like Jesus was able to do certain superhuman things according to the bible, like walking over water or turning water to wine. Both have been resurrected from the death to achieve the ultimate state of their function. Neo's real name "Thomas Anderson" also has biblical roots. "Thomas" is a reference to Jesus' disciple Thomas (comp Kapell 190), who wouldn't belief Jesus' resurrection and consequently represents Neo's doubt towards being "the One". "Anderson" is Greek for "Son of Man", a term that Jesus has often been referred to (comp Kapell 190). "Trinity" refers to the holy trinity in the bible, with Morpheus being the father, Neo being the son and Trinity being the holy ghost (comp Lawrence 206). Cypher seems to be the pendant to Judas Iscariot, the traitor, but he is much more a metaphor for the devil (comp Kapell 191). First of all his name "Cypher" comes from "Lucifer" (comp Kapell 191) and second of all, he serves as Neo's seducer, like the devil did with Jesus in the desert (Mt 4,1-11). In *The Matrix* Cypher tries to convince Neo that the path of following Morpheus is wrong ("Why, oh, why, didn't I take the blue pill?" min 59), just like the devil tried to convince Jesus that following God would be wrong. Also Cypher's appearance reminds of how the devil is portrayed, with a Goatee and red clothes. Last but not least, the name of the last human city Zion and Morpheus' hovercraft ship Nebuchadnezzar are references to the bible. Zion is considered the city of God, where "those in need and in trouble find refuge in" (Lawrence 213) and Nebuchadnezzar was a king in the bible, who suffered from nightmares (comp Lawrence 211).

4.2. Plato's "Allegory of the Cave"

One of the most essential philosophical thoughts is Plato's "Allegory of the Cave". It explains philosophy itself and what goals it follows and *The Matrix* is often cited as having strong parallels to this allegory. It describes a setting, where several people are tied to posts in a cave for their entire life and everything they can see is the wall in front of them. Their captors behind them use several objects and a fire to project shadows of these objects on the wall. Since they never witnessed anything else than the shadows in this cave, they hold them for reality and live unknowingly that there is also a world outside of this cave (comp Lawrence 4). This story can be compared to *The Matrix*: the people tied to the posts are the humans connected to the Matrix, the shadows on the wall are the Matrix and the captors are the Machines. In a philosophical context, the allegory and consequently also *The Matrix*, are a metaphor for the first goal of philosophy: to leave the cave of ignorance and witness the ultimate reality, for we are all in the cave and don't know what reality is really like, with philosophy as the key to leave the cave.

4.3. Other mentionable References

There are a lot of references to Lewis' Carroll's franchise *Alice in Wonderland*. First of all, there are parallels in the setting: both tales tell the story of two parallel existing worlds, *Alice in Wonderland* has the real world and Wonderland and *The Matrix* parallel has the Matrix and the real world. Neo is instructed to "follow the white Rabbit"(min 7) at the beginning of the film. In *Alice's Adventures in Wonderland* the protagonist Alice follows a white, talking rabbit down a rabbit hole into Wonderland. The "rabbit hole" is also mentioned in *The Matrix*, when Morpheus says "You take the red pill, you stay in Wonderland and I show you how deep the rabbit hole goes."(min 28). There is also a reference to the *Alice* sequel *Through the Looking-Glass*, where Alice once again enters a parallel world through a mirror. Shortly before Neo wakes up in the real world, he also witnesses a mirror in the Matrix, that shows an unusual behavior and he gets literally sucked into that mirror.

Next to this, there are other minor references of all kinds. For example, if you look at the name "Neo", you can see, that it is an anagram of "One". Morpheus name derives from the Greek "god of dreams" (Lawrence 203). Matrix literally means "womb"(Lawrence 210) and everyone connected to the Matrix is seen in a womb like booth, filled with liquid. Cypher's real name is Mr. Regan, as a reference to Ronald Reagan. When he makes the deal with an agent, he also wants to be famous and rich as an actor in the Matrix, while Ronald Reagan started his career as an actor, too (comp Lawrence 204). Last but not least, the Oracle is a reference to the Oracle in Delphi, who "was famous for giving good, but difficult to comprehend, advice"(Kapell 196). Like this Oracle in Delphi, the Matrix' Oracle does never give a clear answer, although her advices are crucial for Neo. The Oracle in Delphi had also the words "Know Thyself" engraved on a "nearby temple wall"(Lawrence 70) in Greek, while the Matrix' Oracle has those words written in her kitchen in Latin.

To cut a long story short, almost everything and every name has a certain meaning within *The Matrix* and it depends on the viewer, to decipher all of them.

5. Conclusion

Now you should have a solid idea about how much the movie offers apart from special effects and the typical Hollywood portrayal. You should have a better idea of how the Matrix works and that it contains a lot of references. But you should also know, that it doesn't end here. Like it was said in the Introduction already, this seminar paper only gives you a glimpse of how much *The Matrix* has to offer. There is enough material to fill entire books full of interesting theories about every corner and aspect of the Matrix and yet the film is comprehensible for almost everyone. Also the sequels plus the rest of the franchise could completely re-define the meaning of the Matrix, for they are providing additional information about it. This is what makes *The Matrix* a special movie, because it shows, how even a seemingly plain Hollywood movie, which success was almost entirely driven by action sequences and special effects can define a whole generation of moviegoers through the interest in the unknown.

6. Works Cited

Primary Sources:

The Matrix. Dir. Andy Wachowski and Larry Wachowski. Perf. Keanu Reeves,
Laurence Fishburne. Warner Bros., 1999. DVD.

Secondary Sources:

Lawrence, Matt. *Like a Splinter in Your Mind: The Philosophy behind the Matrix
Trilogy* / Matt Lawrence. Malden, MA: Blackwell Pub., 2004. Print.

Kapell, Matthew, and William G. Doty, eds. *Jacking in to the Matrix Franchise:
Cultural Reception and Interpretation*. New York: Continuum, 2004. Print.

"The MATRIX 101." *The MATRIX 101 - Understanding The Matrix - Symbolism*. N.p.,
n.d. Web. 05 Nov. 2012. <http://www.thematrix101.com/matrix/symbolism.php>.